HOW DO I KILL
REMAINING SIN?

GEOFFREY THOMAS

REFORMATION HERITAGE BOOKS
GRAND RAPIDS, MICHIGAN

How Do I Kill Remaining Sin?
© 2014 by Geoffrey Thomas

All rights reserved. No part of this book may be used or reproduced in any manner whatsoever without written permission except in the case of brief quotations embodied in critical articles and reviews. Direct your requests to the publisher at the following address:

Reformation Heritage Books
2965 Leonard St. NE
Grand Rapids, MI 49525
616-977-0889 / Fax 616-285-3246
orders@heritagebooks.org
www.heritagebooks.org

Printed in the United States of America
15 16 17 18 19 20/10 9 8 7 6 5 4 3 2

ISBN 978-1-60178-308-0

For additional Reformed literature, request a free book list from Reformation Heritage Books at the above regular or e-mail address.

HOW DO I KILL
REMAINING SIN?

———————✖———————

"If ye through the Spirit do mortify the deeds of the body, ye shall live" (Rom. 8:13). What does the word *mortify* mean? You are all familiar with a mortuary, the place to which the dead are consigned. We are speaking about how we as Christians consign or put our sinful natures to death. This is a misunderstood and neglected theme. Its neglect has weakened Christian testimony and dumbed down Christian living. Even Christian worship is affected because of an absence from our services of exhortations to every worshiper to be mortifying or putting to death the remains of sin.

One unconsidered result of this failure to put remaining sin to death is that we find ourselves living in the age of the addict. We have invited technology into our front rooms and have gained the ways and means to indulge our desires. We are witnessing a change in the relationship of people to their social environment. Men have learned the art of manipulating their brains to produce bursts of short-term pleasure. Insidious, life-sapping addictions are common: addictions to sugar, television, alcohol, gambling, credit cards, computer games, drugs, rock music, pornography, and even twenty-four-hour news. All this is rooted in our spiritual malaise. Men have turned from God to "the pleasures of sin for a season," and they have little power to control it.

This is one of the most crucial themes for a Christian to consider. We all need to understand this subject of mortification and to put ourselves under the sanctifying power of God's truth to help us become more mature Christians. Let us consider some biblical propositions that lay a foundation for practical ways of putting to death indwelling sin.

EVERY UNBELIEVER IS DEAD IN TRESPASSES AND SINS

In the eyes of God, every unregenerate man and woman is already dead. Scripture is not reluctant to use this concept. This is the divine diagnosis of the state of man. Ephesians 2 begins, "*You*...were dead in trespasses and sins" (v. 1), and this section ends in verse 5, repeating the same phrase but casting it in the first person plural, "*we* were dead in sins"—"me, too," says the apostle (emphasis added). In other words, there was a time when we Christians were just like the world and totally devoid of the life of heaven—eternal, divine life. Between the bookends of those two declarations of our previous state of death, the apostle explains what he means: we showed that we were dead by living "according to the course of this world" (v. 2a). We were dead fish drifting with the stream; we did and said what everyone else did and said. We followed "the prince of the power of the air, the spirit that now worketh in the children of disobedience" (v. 2b). In other words, we were dominated by Satan. From day to day, we followed the dictates and drives of our fallen, carnal selves, "fulfilling the desires of the flesh and of the mind" (v. 3). The flesh and its demands dominated our lives. That is what it means spiritually to be dead to all the glorious life of God—Father, Son, and Holy Spirit. It is a common theme in the Bible. In Colossians 2:13, Paul likewise reminds his readers that at one time they were dead in their sins. Writing to Timothy about his pastoral care of the women in his church, Paul says bluntly, "She that liveth in pleasure is dead while she liveth" (1 Tim. 5:6).

If you are hesitant about confessing Christ, the problem you face is not a lack of information. Your problem is an utter lack of inner spiritual life! While you are dead, you cannot come to Christ. You need to be drawn to Christ by the Father. You need to be quickened or made alive by the Spirit. So cry with all your heart to God to give you such life from heaven, as well as both the grace to repent and the power to believe. This present life is death without it! Everyone without Christ is dead in sin.

Another proposition follows about a different kind of death, a death in Christ.

EVERY CHRISTIAN IS DEAD TO THE DOMINION OF SIN AND DEATH

What does God do when He makes someone a Christian? What happens when we are joined to Christ by a true faith? Addressing his Christian readers, Paul declares, "Ye are dead, and your life is hid with Christ in God" (Col. 3:3). In another place he says, "How shall we, that are dead to sin, live any longer therein?" (Rom. 6:2). He tells them in the next verses that they—that is, their old selves or sinful natures—have been crucified with Christ, buried with Him, and raised with Him to newness of life. So he exhorts them to count themselves "dead indeed unto sin, but alive unto God through Jesus Christ our Lord" (v. 11).

What is Paul doing here? He is teaching us the doctrine of *definitive mortification, that is, an experience of death that defines us as Christians*. Let me explain this idea.

The Christian is a sinner who has died with Christ. Paul is not telling us to be dead; he is not urging Christians to die; and in this place he is not enforcing any obligation to put sin to death. There is no demand here; Paul is making a simple indicative statement of what is true of all believers: they have died with Christ. Paul is not even saying, "You are dying." That, too, is a biblical truth—believers are dying to sin, that is, they should be mortifying the sin that remains in their members. But that is not the truth that is taught here, because what is before us here is not a process of dying but the fact of death.

The apostle is not describing a line but a point, a definite moment that occurs when the believer is joined to Christ by a true faith. Christ died, and every Christian has died with Him. They are not dying; they have died. In the life of every Christian, there has already occurred the event of death, a definitive mortification, a once-for-all, irreversible actuality.

What does Paul mean? He tells us in Romans 6 that the believer has died to sin. He has not died to the influence of sin, but he has died to the dominion of sin. Sin still works in the believer, but sin does not reign in him. Paul's exhortation is not simply, "Don't let sin reign." He makes the categorical assertion that sin shall not reign (Rom. 6:14). It is impossible for sin to reign in any believer. We are not slaves to sin. Sin orders us: "Don't trust in Jesus Christ! Pour contempt on Calvary! Stop going to church. Stop praying. Don't give God a single thought!" But now that we are born again, we refuse to obey. We cannot obey.

We used to obey the orders or motions of sin, as does the unbelieving world. We said, "Yes, sir," as we cowered before sin and did what sin told us to do, ignoring Jesus Christ and His salvation. We were slaves and prisoners to sin. The great biblical indictment is this: "the scripture hath concluded [shut up or imprisoned] all under sin" (Gal. 3:22). Sin exercises tyranny over the life of the world, so that there is nothing in the lives of lost men and women but sin. An unbeliever is incapable of saying to God: "I do this for Thy sake, because I love Thee and love my neighbor as myself. I do it to Thy glory." He cannot obey God at all, for "without faith it is impossible to please him" (Heb. 11:6; cf. Rom. 14:23).

Only the man or woman who is joined to Christ is capable of real obedience, though he or she cannot yet offer God perfect obedience. Paul here is referring to a definitive moment when the Christian died to sin, when he, by the grace of God, shook off and ended the tyranny of sin. The apostle is saying, "Please try to appreciate the tremendous change that has taken place in your lives, that you who were previously totally averse to all that was godly are now capable, by the Spirit's grace, of the real obedience of Christian faith."

The killing work of God in our lives by uniting us to Christ in His death on the cross means, as Paul says in Colossians 3:9, that we "have put off the old man." We are not simply dying; we have already died. We have broken away from the old man once and for all. However, Paul does not mean that we are finished with remaining or indwelling sin. He recognized that the power of sin continued to work in his own life (Rom. 7:14–25). The good that he would do he did not do, and the evil that he would not do he found himself doing, so he cried out: "O wretched man that I am! who shall deliver me from the body of this death?" (v. 24). But Paul knew something else, too, something wonderful to him and enormously inspirational to us—that the man he once was as the unregenerate persecutor of the church and the unbelieving blasphemer of Christ had ceased to be. The Jesus-hating Pharisees would go on searching for the old Saul of Tarsus, but that Christ-despiser was no more to be found.

We can indict all the sin of which we are conscious in ourselves—how weak and inconsistent we are, how prone to all kinds of temptation—but whatever our failings, we are not the men or women that we used to be. The unregenerate man, dead in sins, has ceased to be. The carnal mind that was enmity against God has ceased to exist. The "natural man" (1 Cor. 2:14), who was totally incapable of receiving the things of the Spirit of God, has ceased to be. The man who was dead in trespasses and sins is no more. The believer is not unregenerate and regenerate at the same time. He does not have a new heart as well as an old heart. He is a regenerate man only. He has only one human nature that has been transformed by the grace of Almighty God. The man dead in sins is the carnal man or the unregenerate man. That old man is dead and gone in the case of the believer. This is definitive mortification. Our regeneration and our union with Jesus Christ by faith represent a decisive break with what we used to be. Every Christian has died to the domination and tyranny of sin.

EVERY CHRISTIAN HAS TO DEAL WITH THE CONSTANT PRESENCE OF THE FLESH

God could have removed sin completely from us when He regenerated us. He did much for us at that time, far above all that we asked or even thought! He has freely given each believer all things with Christ. Before we knew what we needed from Him, He gave us total forgiveness for our sins—past, present, and future. He credited to our account all the perfect righteousness of our Lord and the merit of His perfect obedience, even to the death of the cross. Moreover, God put a new spirit within us. He gave us saving trust in Himself and in His Son. He gave us a new Master and ended the tyranny of sin over us. He gave us the privilege of adoption into His family. He gave us a glorious inheritance, making us co-heirs with Jesus the Son of God.[1]

He joined us to Christ, just as a branch is grafted to a vine, so that the life of Christ can flow into us. He gave us the baptism of the Holy Spirit, so that by one Spirit we were all baptized into one body. He gave us the Holy Spirit to seal us as His people and to confirm the promise of our future inheritance until the day of Christ. He then seated us in the heavenly places in Jesus Christ to affirm our eternal status as sons of God and co-heirs with Christ. He promised that from that moment on He would supply all our needs and ensure that all things would work together for our good. He will allow nothing to separate us from His love.[2]

---

1. Col. 2:13; Rom. 4:3, 23–25; 5:18–19; Ezek. 36:25–27; Rom. 8:15–17.
2. John 15:5; 1 Cor. 12:12–13; Eph. 1:13–14; 2:6; Phil. 4:19; Rom. 8:28, 39.

Our life in Christ reveals continually, one truth at a time, that in having Christ, we have all things. God didn't explain to us what we needed as the years went by, only to make us wait and agonize and intercede until finally He grudgingly gave us some meager portion as our blessing. No, He has already blessed us with every spiritual blessing in the heavenly places in Christ. He dealt with us in grace, not according to our merit or understanding. But one thing He did not do, and that was to make us perfect in holiness, even though He could have. He has reserved complete Christlikeness until the moment when we will meet the Lord Jesus Christ face to face. When we see Him, we will be like Him, but not before. Until then, conformity to Christ is the goal set before us toward which we must strive daily, aiming for progressive sanctification through progressive mortification.

Scripture also reveals that we Christians must confront the remnants of sin within us. The consequence is strife, or spiritual warfare. This conflict is described in Galatians 5:16–17: "This I say then, Walk in the Spirit, and ye shall not fulfil the lust of the flesh. For the flesh lusteth against the Spirit, and the Spirit against the flesh: and these are contrary the one to the other: so that ye cannot do the things that ye would." Our flesh is fed up with existing alongside our renewed spiritual nature, but the two are conjoined. For the present, my flesh (remaining sin) and my spirit are bound together. There is no separation and no possibility of a truce. There is ongoing war. The flesh always tries to prevent our obedience, trip us up, turn down the thermostats of our hearts so that they grow cold, put stumbling blocks in front of us, encourage resentful thoughts of others, make us bitter, and cause us to justify our failings as disciples. Through this ongoing conflict, we realize that we cannot obey God perfectly as we desire to do.

This conflict is described poignantly in Romans 7: "For that which I do I allow not [know or approve not]: for what I would, that do I not; but what I hate, that do I" (v. 15). Paul adds: "For I know that in me (that is, in my flesh,) dwelleth no good thing: for to will is present with me; but how to perform that which is good I find not. For the good that I would I do not: but the evil which I would not, that I do" (vv. 18–19). He says again: "I find then a law, that, when I would do good, evil is present with me. For I delight in the law of God after the inward man: but I see another law in my members, warring against the law of my mind, and bringing me into captivity to the law of sin which is in my members" (vv. 21–23). James describes our failures in this fight like this: "Every man is tempted, when he is drawn away of his own lust, and enticed. Then when lust hath conceived, it bringeth forth sin: and sin, when it is finished, bringeth forth death" (1:14–15).

This battle will not end until we look upon the face of our glorified Savior. Face up to this reality. Know your enemy. Don't be surprised by his assaults. Know yourself. The sins in others that disgust you the most exist in seed form in you. Those evil actions that make you draw in your breath and say, "How could anyone do something like that?"—the seed of those sins is in your life, and could begin to grow, if you are not at pains to root it out.

Because of this conflict, the Lord and His servants exhort us: "Watch and pray! Put on all the armor of God! Awake! Don't slumber on like others! Stand in an evil day, and having done all, stand! Yield not to temptation!"[3] Christ exhorts His disciples because of the danger from the enemy within, as well as the enemy without.

There have been religious movements that have promised short cuts to ending the fight between the Spirit and the flesh. A hundred years, ago there was a teaching known as the Victorious Life. One of its proponents, Charles Trumbull, wrote, "I have learned that, as I trust Christ for surrender, there need be no fighting against sin, but complete freedom from the power, and even the desire of sin."[4] What an error! No preacher possesses a secret by which we can escape from the activity of sin within us. Modest, respectable, and quiet sin can be every bit as dangerous as roaring, spitting, and shouting sin. Sin is never

---

3. Matt. 26:41; Luke 21:36; Rom. 13:11–14; Eph. 6:10–13, 18; 1 Thess. 5:6–8; Col. 4:2.

4. Charles Trumbull, *Victory in Christ* (Philadelphia: Sunday School Times Co., 1923), chap. 2, http://www.abidingabove.org/downloads/suggested-reading/VictoryInChrist-CharlesTrumbull.pdf.

less active than when it is most silent. When sin is quiet, we are to be most on guard.

Dr. Cornelius Van Til was one of my teachers at Westminster Theological Seminary in Philadelphia. He was in his seventies when he taught me. There was once a student conference at our campus, and the InterVarsity Christian Fellowship groups from the Philadelphia universities came. There was a question-and-answer session at the end. A student asked, "Dr. Van Til, isn't there a sense in which as you get older, sins that once bothered you no longer do so?" Van Til, his finger shaking, answered energetically, "Young man, that is incipient perfectionism. The greatest battles I fight now are the same battles I fought as a student." The fight never ends, and we must fight on to our deathbeds.

You will sympathize when a new Christian says to you one day, "Before I was a Christian, in some ways, things seemed easier. Now I find I've got new problems; I find myself at war with myself." You should say, "Praise the Lord!" You should be glad to hear that, because that is how it should be. That is the mark of the activity of the Holy Spirit in a Christian's life. He challenges the corrupt patterns of our lives that went unchallenged before we were born of the Spirit. Of course, life had to be easier psychologically before our conversions. There was no indwelling Spirit. We could sing, "I did it my way." There was no pressure on us from God the Holy Spirit to change our sinful attitudes and ways. Once we are "born from above" (John 3:7, KJV marginal note), immediately our flesh no longer has its way, and it lashes out and kicks against us. We do have new problems, for now the Spirit commences an internal war against sin.

EVERY CHRISTIAN IS TO BE CONSTANTLY KILLING REMAINING SIN

In the King James Version of the Bible, the word *mortify* appears in Romans 8:13: "If ye through the Spirit do mortify the deeds of the body, ye shall live." There is just one other place where this word appears. In Colossians 3:5, Paul exhorts his readers, "Mortify therefore your members which are upon the earth; fornication, uncleanness, inordinate affection, evil concupiscence, and covetousness, which is idolatry." You ask, "Are there really only two places in the KJV where the term *mortify* is found?" Yes, but let us not think that this means mortification is an optional activity referred to only in a few bypaths in Scripture.

The Old Testament, for example, teaches this duty when David says in his prayer, "The sacrifices of God are a broken spirit: a broken and a contrite heart, O God, thou wilt not despise" (Ps. 51:17). Such broken, contrite hearts and spirits are fruits of mortification. David knew that remaining sin makes us proud. It tells us to ignore God and to do things our way. As a penitent believer, David's heart and spirit had been broken by the knowledge that, even as a child of God, he was still capable of committing grievous sins (adultery, murder, gross deception) against his God. Likewise, David prays in Psalm 141:3–4: "Set a watch, O LORD, before my mouth; keep the door of my lips. Incline not my heart to any evil thing." In other words, he wanted God to put the brakes on his remaining propensity for sin! That was David's prayer—that he would be helped to fight against the flesh. Mortification of sin appears in the Psalms frequently.

Our Lord Jesus teaches us about battling against remaining sin. He disdains the Pharisees' obsession with outward ritual, such as washing their hands ceremonially before every meal. Christ says:

> Do not ye yet understand, that whatsoever entereth in at the mouth goeth into the belly, and is cast out into the draught? But those things which proceed out of the mouth come forth from the heart; and they defile the man. For out of the heart proceed evil thoughts, murders, adulteries, fornications, thefts, false witness, blasphemies: these are the things which defile a man: but to eat with unwashen [unwashed] hands defileth not a man. (Matt. 15:17–20)

Our problem is internal, He tells us, and we must think zealously about this fact rather than dwell on external things. Such things do not belong to the essence of true religion, but are the sum and substance of false religion. We have to deal with the flesh, because if we don't deal with it, it's going to deal with us, increasingly and powerfully, striving to gain the mastery over us. It will make us unclean, that is, impure, defiled, and unfit for communion with God, if we don't control it.

Jesus addresses the need to mortify remaining sin in the Sermon on the Mount:

> Ye have heard that it was said by them of old time, Thou shalt not commit adultery: but I say unto you, That whosoever looketh on a woman to lust after her hath committed adultery with her already in his heart. And if thy right eye offend thee, pluck it out, and cast it from thee: for it is profitable for thee that one of thy members should perish, and not that thy whole body should be cast into hell. And if thy right hand offend thee, cut it off, and cast it from thee: for it is profitable for thee that one of thy members should perish, and not that thy whole body should be cast into hell. (Matt. 5:27–30)

The picture is of a diseased eye or a gangrenous limb; if it is not amputated, the disease will spread and destroy the body.

It must be noted that the Lord is not telling us to mutilate our bodies; that would be a grievous sin against the sixth commandment ("Thou shalt not kill"), which requires us to protect and preserve our bodies, and not harm them. Jesus is using graphic but figurative language, urging us to be merciless in denying ourselves and battling the lusts of the flesh, so that we may lay hold of eternal life, be useful in the church, and promote the glory of God. The alternative is go on in sin and end up in hell, or, as Paul says, "be a castaway" (1 Cor. 9:27), that is, someone who has made shipwreck in the journey of life.

In plain terms, our Lord is urging us to rid ourselves of anything that accommodates the lusts of the flesh or enables us to fulfill them. He commands us to do whatever we can do to fortify ourselves against temptation and to separate ourselves from our sins, lest they separate us from God. "Put ye on the Lord Jesus Christ, and make not provision for the flesh, to fulfil the lusts thereof" (Rom. 13:14). Notice that it's not just any hand or eye that Jesus speaks of. It's the right hand and the right eye; for most people, the right hand is the most important one, the stronger or more adroit member, often a source of pride and self-confidence. Even our strengths can become weaknesses when they are put in the service of sin and the flesh. In other words, there may be things good in themselves, or at least things indifferent, that are accommodating and enabling sin in our lives in one way or other. Whether it is the books we read, the entertainment we watch, or the leisure-time pursuits we enjoy, if these things come into conflict with the loyalty and love we owe to God alone or become adjuncts and avenues of any other kind of sin, we must part with them for Christ's sake.

Let's apply this teaching to a variety of problems that even Christians can struggle with.

Drunkenness
Drunkenness is both sinful and destructive; accord-

ing to Paul, drunkards (among many other kinds of sinners) shall not inherit the kingdom of God (1 Cor. 6:9, 10). Here's a man who has habitually struggled with alcohol, but now places his faith in Jesus Christ. He finds in the Savior forgiveness for his drunkenness (1 Cor. 6:11). You've become his friend as a fellow believer, and you want to help him. You should tell him: "You have to avoid every contact with that old way of life. When you come to church, don't take the way that passes by the bar you used to visit. Avoid that street; come another route. In the supermarket, don't go down the aisle with the bottles of liquor. Imagine that you no longer have a hand to reach out for a glass of whiskey; you've cut it off. You no longer have an eye to see the bottles. You don't have a nose to smell the stuff. You don't have feet to walk there. Don't even think of meeting with the old crowd."

Remind him that we are all influenced by the company we keep, and, as Paul says, "Evil communications [associations with evildoers] corrupt good manners" (1 Cor. 15:33). He has to break off contact with old friends and drinking buddies because their influence will counteract all that the gospel has been teaching him. Rather, he needs to build positive relationships with the people who are going to help him in striving against the power of alcohol in his life and in solving the problem of abusing alcohol and abusing his body.

You should advise him: "Come to the men's

breakfast at our church. Be at the prayer meeting each week, and we'll pray for you, and you can tell God there in the presence of us all how hard it is, and we will weep with you when you fall. We will be your friends and we will do things together." In so doing, you can help such a man to "cut off the hand" that holds the whiskey glass. That is one case of putting sin to death.

Adultery

Here's a Christian who's stumbled badly and been unfaithful to his wife. Like drunkenness, adultery is deadly sin (1 Cor. 6:9–10; Rev. 21:8). Let's apply Jesus' teaching on mortification to his situation by examining it in the light of Scripture. Assuming that his wife is willing to forgive him and be reconciled to him, you must urge him to repent of any and all behaviors that enabled him to indulge his carnal desires and look for affection, romance, and sexual pleasure in the arms of another woman.

These behaviors include the fantasies he has harbored and indulged; the pornography with which he has fed his lusts; the dirty jokes he has told or laughed at; the flirtations he has engaged in and the liberties he has taken with other women (behaviors he once wrote off as harmless); the self-esteem he has derived from his own estimate of his sexual attractiveness and prowess; and the low view of marriage and the marriage covenant he has absorbed from the culture around him. He must change the way he thinks about love, sex, and marriage. He must rid himself of any practices or habits that undermine or endanger the love and loyalty he owes to his wife. He must break off any improper relationships he has with other women, discarding phone numbers, destroying trophies and mementos, and ceasing to have any private meetings or personal correspondence with them. Sad to say, in these days, this means he may have to quit his job and seek other employment, since the modern mind tolerates fornication and adultery in the workplace. Above all else, he must learn the wisdom of rejoicing with "the wife of [his] youth" and being "ravished always with her love" (Prov. 5:18–19).

Pornography
Here is a man whose problem is Internet pornography. Scores of millions of people every year visit porn sites, and soon the figure will be hundreds of millions as the developing world hooks up to the Internet. The images they look at are shockingly explicit. Never before in human history have so many middle-class people discovered how powerfully sin is active in their hearts. Internet pornography is the quick road to addiction. Those who look at it are like alcoholics taking their first drink. They have no idea where they will end up, but many of them scarcely care.

We care! We say to them what Paul said to the Philippian jailer, "Do thyself no harm" (Acts 16:28). Then we tell the gospel to all who hear us, and we pray for them to have new hearts and to know the power of the Holy Spirit in their lives, a new energy and strength to resist. We long for them to know what Thomas Chalmers called "the expulsive power of a new affection," that is, the power of love for Jesus to drive out evil desires as we choose to love and serve Him most of all every day in every way.[5]

We teach the man watching Internet pornography that mortifying or killing remaining sin is the only way of deliverance. We teach him that it is indispensable for his eternal good, and we offer him help to do it. We meet with him weekly for counsel. We say quietly to him on Sundays, "Had a good week?" He knows what we are asking, and he just nods or shrugs. We tell him about a program on the web called Covenant Eyes that he might join. A result of his joining this program is that the heading of every website he visits in a week is sent to us, and he goes to his laptop and smartphone knowing that we will know what he is watching and he will be accountable to us.[6]

The choice, I tell you, is very stark; it is either addiction or it is mortification by the Spirit. Mortification means that things that are most valuable to you may have to go. You may need to change your

---

5. Thomas Chalmers, "The Expulsive Power of a New Affection," in *The Works of Thomas Chalmers* (Glasgow: William Collins, 1836), 6:209–33; "Lectures on the Epistle of Paul the Apostle to the Romans," in *Works*, 23:75.

6. www.covenanteyes.com.

job or move to a different community. Will it be addiction or mortification? Perhaps there is something that means more to you than anything else that may have to go. I knew a man who told me that he had given up his photography hobby and sold all his cameras and equipment. It had become an idol and a snare to him. I questioned whether it was necessary, but I couldn't dissuade him. This is the kind of action for which Jesus is calling. It's definitive. It's once for all. All the things you utilize to enable you to sin have to go. You're not going to get them back.

Addiction to pornography is akin to dabbling in the dark arts of the occult, magic, mysticism, Satanism, spiritism, necromancy, fortune-telling, palmistry, astrology, and so on. These are forms of counterfeit spirituality, superstition, and false religion to which men have resorted as an alternative to calling on the name of the Lord and trusting in His Word. By these "works of darkness," many have been defiled, and Christians should have nothing to do with them (Eph. 5:11). But across the centuries, some professing to be believers have involved themselves with the occult in various ways. Acts 19 records what happened when seven Jewish exorcists, the sons of Sceva, attempted to conjure an evil spirit "by Jesus whom Paul preacheth" (v. 13). The violent response of the evil spirit terrified and humbled the whole city, including many members of the Christian church in that place: "Many that believed came, and confessed, and shewed their deeds. Many of them also which used curious arts [occult practices] brought their books together, and burned them before all men: and they counted the price of them, and found it fifty thousand pieces of silver" (vv. 18–19). What an example of true repentance, in terms of both right motivation (the fear of God) and willingness to incur great financial loss to have done with such detestable sins!

For deliverance, there has to be such single-minded commitment to putting to death remaining sin. Let me illustrate this through the experience of a pastor named Conrad Murrell in his own words:

> A few years ago a pastor brought a troubled man to me for counseling. When I asked him about his problem, he replied, "I want to serve the Lord but I am having a terrible time."
>
> "What seems to be hindering you?" I asked.
>
> "Everything and everybody it seems," he said.
>
> "Let's get down to particulars," I insisted.
>
> This is his story: "I have a smoking problem. I know I shouldn't be smoking. It is harmful to me and a blight on my testimony but I am having a hard time giving it up. Then there is my wife. She thinks I am a fanatic and she says if I insist on living a Christian life, she is going to leave me. She wants to have some fun, and I don't want to go back into that kind of life; but I don't want to lose my wife.
>
> "Then there is my business partner. He is not a Christian and we are having a conflict over some unethical business deals he wants to pull. He says I am holding back the business with my stupid morals and if I don't shape up he is going to force me out.

"Then, last week I was down in Tucson in a restaurant feeling sorry for myself and this young divorcee approached me. She liked me and made some obvious suggestions and approaches. I almost fell into what she was proposing. But I don't want to live like that. I'm just in a terrible mess."

"You surely are," I said, "but, maybe I can help you get some things settled. It seems to me you have about four options here. You can only take one of them so you may as well eliminate the other three. Let's find out which ones you can take and which ones you cannot and then see what we have left. Here is your first option. You can walk out that door the same way you came in with nothing changed and nothing settled. Can you do that?"

"I don't want to."

"But can you?"

"If I had not wanted help I would not have come here."

"But can you leave without it? Are you willing to walk out of here the same way you came in? Can you do that? Can you go on living the way you are now? Think about it. Because if you can, you will. There is no use of me wrangling around here with you for two or three hours only to have you refuse to do what you must and leave the same way you came in. If you can do that, then go ahead and do it now. Let's not waste any more time."

He looked at me, saw I meant it, thought about it a bit and then said, "No, I can't do that. I have got to have some help. I cannot live any longer the way I am. Something has to be settled."

"Then we can eliminate that option. It no longer exists. Something has to be settled before you leave here tonight. Now we have only three left. Here is your second option: forget about being a Christian and forget about mortifying sin. Put the thought of it out of your mind and go ahead and do what you like. If you want to smoke, stop feeling guilty about it and puff away. If your wife wants you to go out and get drunk with her, go ahead. If your partner wants to pull some fast deals that can make you rich and won't get you in jail, go for it. Take advantage of anybody you can, make as much money as you can, do what you like and live it up. If you see that divorcee again, take her up on the proposition. Whatever you feel like doing, help yourself."

He stared at me incredulously, wondering was I serious.

"Can you do that?" I asked.

He shook his head, "No, I can't do that. I can't live that way."

"Are you sure?"

"I'm sure."

"Think about it now and settle it. If you can do that then you ought to go ahead because you will sooner or later. But if you can't, then settle it in your mind that you can't and forget about it. It's no use you ever thinking about it anymore. It is an utter impossibility."

He replied, "I can't do that."

"All right, that eliminates two options and two more are left, here is your third one: Go home. If you do not have one at home, stop off at a pawn shop and pick yourself up a pistol. Get out in the yard so that you won't make a mess in the house for someone to clean up, take good aim so that you don't miss, and put a bullet in your brain."

He jerked his head back and stared at me. "No, I can't do that."

"Then it looks like you have only one course left. Follow the Lord and declare war on your sins without surrender. If your wife leaves you, follow the Lord. If you lose your business and all your money, follow the Lord. If it costs you all your pleasures, put to death remaining sin. You really don't have any other option. You cannot do anything else. Live, die, swim, or sink, you must follow the Lord and keep killing your sins."

He thought awhile, then lifted his head and slowly, as the truth began to dawn upon him, a relieved smile spread across his worried face. "That's right, isn't it? It's really very simple. He is my only hope of life. There is nothing else to do." I prayed with him, shook his hand and dismissed the meeting.

Nearly two years later I was back in the same city and this man came to the meeting. His wife was with him, clinging to his arm. They had been, it seemed, through the toughest time of their marriage. His faith had been tried in the fire. The devil had exhausted his resources in his attempt to shake him from the commitment he made that night. But when he had left that counseling session, he was a single-minded man with only one place to go. His eyes were steadfastly fixed upon God as his deliverer and sin as his enemy. He and his wife both wore the broad sweet smiles of a victory that endures. They had learned indeed that faith is the victory that overcomes the world. Such as these can give unerring testimony that God is indeed worthy of our trust.[7]

That is mortification.

PUTTING TO DEATH REMAINING SIN MUST ALWAYS BE ACCOMPANIED BY LOOKING UNTO JESUS

Mortification is only half of the Christian's battle with sin. Mortification is not *the* secret to the Christian life. It is a danger, I suppose, when we first discover it, to imagine that it is. The truth of mortification is neglected, and so we who have discovered its importance in the Bible can overemphasize it. Some seem to set out on a mission, proclaiming that mortification is the "silver bullet" of successful discipleship.

We must emphasize the necessity of mortification and apply it to our lives, but only in balance with all other Christian truths that deal with holy and God-honoring living. In Reformed theology, the counterpart to mortification is vivification, the bringing to life of the new man. These parallel benefits that flow to us from the power of Christ and His atoning blood involve both putting sin to death and looking unto and living out of Jesus Christ. They are as inseparable as the two sides of a coin. The Bible teaches likewise that there are two ways to serve God better and grow in honoring Him: one is mortifying the flesh and the other is trusting in Jesus with all your

---

7. Conrad Murrell, *Faith Cometh* (Bentley, La.: Saber Publications, 1976), 35–38.

heart and living out of Him. The one is deadly toward sin, but the other is the very fountain of life for the Christian. Experientially, we need both mortification and vivification if we are truly going to kill sin.

Let's see this in Hebrews 12:1–3. Verse 1 says, "Wherefore seeing we also are compassed about with so great a cloud of witnesses, let us lay aside every weight, and the sin which doth so easily beset us, and let us run with patience the race that is set before us." That is mortification, expressed here in terms of casting off anything that hinders our forward progress.

However, verses 2–3 add:

> Looking unto Jesus the author and finisher of our faith; who for the joy that was set before him endured the cross, despising the shame, and is set down at the right hand of the throne of God. For consider him that endured such contradiction of sinners against himself, lest ye be wearied and faint in your minds.

That is Christ's vivifying grace that enables us to fix our eyes on the Lord Jesus.

Can you see the perfect balance of those two exhortations? "Laying aside very weight" is balanced by "looking unto Jesus." Both are essential. If the Christian life consisted only of cutting off the right hand that offends and plucking out the right eye, keeping under the body and bringing it into subjection (1 Cor. 9:27), and killing remaining lusts, then no doubt in a very short time we would all "be wearied and faint in [our] minds" (Heb. 12:3). Each day would be just one more day of fighting against sin. We would come to feel like Matthew Arnold's character in *Sohrab and Rustum*, when he says:

> But now in blood and battles was my youth
> And full of blood and battles is my age,
> And I shall never end this life of blood.[8]

But the Christian life is not like that. Certainly you shall never cease having to struggle against sin, and you may have to resist even to the point of shedding blood (Heb. 12:4). But there is another delightful and demanding duty that we are to perform, and that is to take hold of our great Savior as our Prophet, Priest, and King. We trust in His promises, we look to Him to supply what we most need when we need it most, and we heed His commands. Every passing moment we look to Him, saying, "Lord, if Thou wilt, Thou canst make me clean." David counsels us to "wait on the LORD: be of good courage, and he shall strengthen thine heart" (Ps. 27:14). The dynamics of the relationship between mortification of sin and trusting in Christ have been made plain to us by Robert Murray M'Cheyne, who urges that "for every look at yourself you take ten looks at the Lord Jesus."[9] "They looked unto him, and were lightened:

---

8. Matthew Arnold, "Sohrab and Rustum," in *Select Poems of Matthew Arnold* (London: William Heinemann, 1905), 1:29.

9. Robert Murray M'Cheyne to George Shaw, Sept. 16, 1840, in *Memoir and Remains*, ed. Andrew A. Bonar (1892; repr., Edinburgh:

and their faces were not ashamed" (Ps. 34:5). We can never look to Him enough.

Joel Beeke speaks of this Christ-centered vivification this way:

> Paul tells us to fight against sin from a position of strength (Rom. 6; Eph. 6). Know what you are in Christ. In Christ we have died unto sin. In Christ we have been raised again to newness of life. In Christ crucified we have been set free from sin's dominion and continue to die to sin, so that, as John Owen emphasizes, we experience the death of sin in the death of Christ. Sin may assail but cannot master us, so long as we stand firm in Christ, calling upon His name. In Christ we are assured of God's help in striving against sin. Though we may fall and lose various skirmishes against sin, because of our union and communion with Christ we have by faith the promise of ultimate victory and final deliverance, which, more than anything else, gives us hope and sustenance in the daily fight against sin. The only sin fatal to our cause is unbelief. Unbelief alone can rob us of God's grace and shut us out of His kingdom.[10]

Looking to Christ does not mean having a picture

Banner of Truth, 1966), 293. It is not clear whom M'Cheyne quoted. Thomas Chalmers had quoted Richard Baxter as saying, "For every thought that he casts downwardly upon himself, he should cast ten upwardly and outwardly upon Jesus, and upon the glorious truths of the gospel" (*Letters of Thomas Chalmers* [Edinburgh: Banner of Truth, 2007], 301), but the exact source of this quote is unknown.

10. Joel R. Beeke, "31 Days of Purity: Putting Sin to Death," *Challies .com*, http://www.challies.com/articles/31-days-of-purity-putting-sin -to-death.

of Him for the eyes to look upon; rather, it means meditating in the heart on what Scripture says about His person and work. Two books are very valuable in this connection, for both sum up and expound the witness of Scripture to Christ. They were both written within a few years of each other by Puritan pastor-preachers. The first was written by Isaac Ambrose and is entitled *Looking unto Jesus*,[11] and the second was written by John Owen and is entitled *The Mortification of Sin*.[12] Ambrose leads us to meditate on Christ's glory in every aspect of His work. Owen gives directions for mortifying sin and says that the grand direction is this: "Set faith at work on Christ for the killing of thy sin. His blood is the great sovereign remedy for sin-sick souls. Live in this, and thou wilt die a conqueror."[13]

---

11. Isaac Ambrose, *Looking unto Jesus: A View of the Everlasting Gospel: or, The Soul's Eyeing of Jesus, As Carrying on the Great Work of Man's Salvation, from First to Last* (1856; repr., Harrisonburg, Va.: Sprinkle Publications, 1986).

12. John Owen, *The Mortification of Sin in Believers*, in *The Works of John Owen* (1850–1853; repr., Edinburgh: Banner of Truth, 1965–1967), 6:1–86. Also available in abridged form as John Owen, *The Mortification of Sin*, Puritan Paperbacks (Edinburgh: Banner of Truth, 2004).

13. Owen, *Mortification*, in *Works*, 6:79.